HADRIAN'S WALL

Dawn Finch

raintree 🍃
a Capstone company — publishers for children

Raintree is an imprint of Capstone Global Library Limited, a company incorporated in England and Wales having its registered office at 264 Banbury Road, Oxford, OX2 7DY – Registered company number: 6695582

www.raintree.co.uk
myorders@raintree.co.uk

Edited by Helen Cox Cannons
Designed by Cynthia Della-Rovere
Original illustrations © Capstone Global Library Limited 2018
Picture research by Tracy Cummins
Production by Laura Manthe
Originated by Capstone Global Library Limited
Printed and bound in India

ISBN 978 1 4747 6329 5
22 21 20 19 18
10 9 8 7 6 5 4 3 2 1

British Library Cataloguing in Publication Data
A full catalogue record for this book is available from the British Library.

Acknowledgements
We would like to thank the following for permission to reproduce photographs:
Alamy: Tim Gainey, 14; Capstone: Eric Gohl, 8; Dawn Finch: 9, 10, 12, 17, 22, 23, 26, 27; Getty Images: DEA/G. NIMATALLAH, 25, Heritage Images, 16, Print Collector/CM Dixon, 11; Newscom: English Heritage/Heritage Images, 13, 20; Shutterstock: David Peter Robinson, 4, ESB Professional, Design Element, happykanppy, Design Element, Julie Smith L'Heureux, Design Element, Klaus Rademaker, Design Element, Mark Mullen, Design Element, mountainpix, 6, mykhailo pavlenko, Design Element, nienora, Design Element, Peter Hermes Furian, 5, Phillip Maguire, Cover, 1, PiXXart, Design Element, S-F, 7, spatuletail, Design Element, Steve Collender, Design Element, Valentin Agapov, Design Element, Vitalii Gaidukov, 15; The Vindolanda Trust, 21.

The author would like to thank Sonya Galloway and the Vindolanda Trust for all their help and support in the preparation of this book.

Contents

Roman Britain: life on the edge of the Roman Empire...4

Who was Hadrian?..................................6

How was Hadrian's Wall built? 8

How do we know about life on Hadrian's Wall? 10

What is a milecastle? 12

Soldiers of the wall..............................14

Letter from a Roman soldier 18

Life for Britons near the wall 20

Letter from a Briton............................24

Hadrian's Wall after the Romans 26

Timeline 28

Glossary 29

Find out more 30

Index 32

Some words appear in this book in bold, **like this**. You can find out what they mean by looking in the glossary.

Roman Britain: life on the edge of the Roman Empire

During the pre-Roman Iron Age (about 800 BC to AD 43), Britain was home to dozens of large tribes. Each of these tribes had its own **territory** and was prepared to defend it. Many of the tribes of Britain were involved in long wars with their neighbours over territories, but many more lived in peace.

CAESAR INVADES BRITAIN

For a long time, the Romans thought of Britain as an unimportant distant land. They did not see the many different tribes in Britain as a **threat** to the Roman Empire. However, in 55 BC there was a change of heart and Julius Caesar **invaded** Britain. The invasion was not successful because tribes in Britain united to fight the Romans. Caesar again tried to invade Britain the following year, arriving with 30,000 soldiers. The Britons fought the Romans bravely. Caesar decided he did not want a long war in Britain so the Roman army returned to Rome.

At the time of the Roman invasion, the people of Britain lived in simple roundhouses like this one.

CLAUDIUS CONQUERS BRITAIN

Nearly 100 years later, in AD 43, **Emperor** Claudius and the Roman army successfully invaded and settled in Britain. After the Romans invaded, their army needed to get around the country quickly to **occupy** and defend their new land. To do this, the Romans built many roads, camps and forts for their soldiers.

In AD 122, Emperor Hadrian visited Britain. He was worried about reports of tribes **rebelling** against the Romans. He ordered a wall to be built along the northern border of the Roman Empire in Britain. This wall was to become known as Hadrian's Wall.

This map shows in red the Roman Empire in AD 117, when it was at its largest. At the time of building Hadrian's Wall, the Roman Empire had over 65 million citizens – that was 21 per cent of the world's population.

5

Who was Hadrian?

Hadrian was born in Spain in AD 76. He was the **emperor** of Rome between AD 117 and AD 138. Hadrian became emperor after the previous emperor, Trajan, died. Hadrian was very close to Trajan and his family – Trajan was his father's cousin. The family raised Hadrian from the age of ten after both his parents died. Hadrian was well educated. From the age of fourteen he received military training and fought for Trajan in battles across the Roman Empire.

THE BORDERS OF THE EMPIRE

Defending the borders of the Roman Empire was dangerous and expensive. As emperor, Hadrian wanted to make sure that the borders of the empire were constantly protected. He had heard many reports of **rebellions** against the Empire, so in AD 121 he set out on a tour of the Roman Empire. This was the first of many tours during his time as emperor.

This is a sculpture of Hadrian.

HADRIAN'S TOUR

On his tour, Hadrian visited the Roman **territories** of Gaul and Germany, then arrived in Britain. He inspected the armies and defences of the **Northern Frontier**, and ordered the building of the wall that is named after him. Hadrian wanted the wall to show the power of the Roman army. The wall would also join up the gaps between existing Roman forts and **defensive structures**.

AN INTERESTING MAN

Hadrian became known for his impressive building projects. During his rule, he ordered the construction of many buildings, including libraries, bath houses, **aqueducts**, theatres and grand villas. He was a great lover of the arts and poetry, and collected ancient Greek art for his homes. He died at his splendid villa in Baiae aged 62.

Fast Fact!

Hadrian's Wall was never meant to be a border between Scotland and England. In fact, people did not think of England and Scotland as being separate countries at that time.

Hadrian was buried in a tomb in a huge building called the Castel Sant'Angelo. It sits on the banks of the Tiber river in Rome.

How was Hadrian's Wall built?

Hadrian's Wall runs from coast to coast across the north of Britain, from the banks of the River Tyne near the North Sea to the Solway Firth on the Irish Sea. It links a system of forts along the Cumbrian coast. The wall took many years to build, and work began in the east and finished in the west. As well as the stone wall, there were milecastles (see page 12) along the route. There was a fort roughly every five Roman miles. The Romans also dug deep ditches and **earthworks** on the southern side of the wall. This was called the **vallum**.

This is a map showing where Hadrian's Wall is. It runs for almost 118 kilometres (73 miles). A Roman mile was 1,000 paces – about 1,481 metres. That is 0.92 of a modern mile.

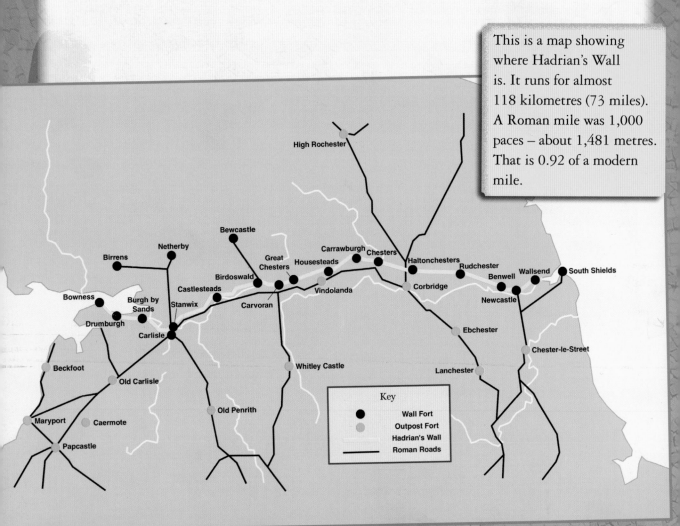

High Rochester

Bewcastle

Netherby

Birrens

Great Chesters

Carrawburgh Chesters

Housesteads

Haltonchesters

Rudchester

Benwell

Wallsend

South Shields

Birdoswald

Castlesteads

Vindolanda

Corbridge

Newcastle

Bowness

Burgh by Sands

Stanwix

Carvoran

Drumburgh

Carlisle

Ebchester

Chester-le-Street

Beckfoot

Whitley Castle

Lanchester

Old Carlisle

Old Penrith

Maryport

Caermote

Papcastle

Key

● Wall Fort
● Outpost Fort
   Hadrian's Wall
— Roman Roads

BUILDING METHODS

Remains of various types of building materials have been found, as the Romans used whatever was available nearby. Early parts of the wall were built of **turf**, stone and wood. Later parts were built only in stone.

To make the most of natural features like ridges of rock, the wall was not built in a straight line, like Roman roads were. This meant that the wall could have better links with existing forts of the **Northern Frontier**, such as the large fort of Vindolanda.

WHO BUILT THE WALL?

Experts think that it would have taken more than 15,000 men to build Hadrian's Wall. Soldiers from all three of the **occupying** Roman **legions** were used to build the wall. As well as the **legionnaires** (members of the legions), there were **auxiliaries**. Extra workers from local tribes were also used.

Fast Fact!

Hadrian's Wall may have been as high as 6 metres and as wide as 3 metres in some places.

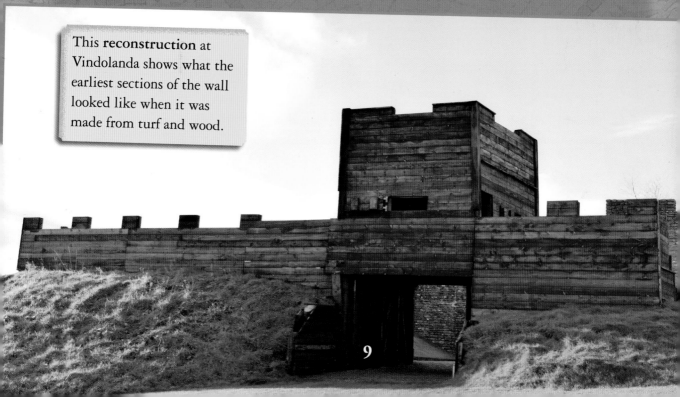

This **reconstruction** at Vindolanda shows what the earliest sections of the wall looked like when it was made from turf and wood.

How do we know about life on Hadrian's Wall?

Hadrian's Wall has been studied by archaeologists for hundreds of years. **Excavations** are still happening today. Only a very small percentage of the wall has been fully excavated, so there is still a lot to learn. But we do have other ways of learning more about the wall's history.

INSCRIPTIONS

There are some very good Roman sources of information, including **inscriptions**. An inscription is a note that has been carved or chiselled on to an object. There are many inscriptions on tombstones that were made by the Romans during their time in Britain. They provide us with a record of the buildings, people and places who were there at the time. These often show who paid for a building, what it was built for and who it was **dedicated** to. Some inscriptions have a date on them.

Inscriptions carved on small **altar** stones like these tell us who paid for them and which gods they were worshipping.

THE VINDOLANDA TABLETS

The most fascinating source of information about life at Hadrian's Wall are the Vindolanda tablets. These are very thin wooden tablets that were written on and used to send messages. They are quite like our modern postcards! Most date from as early as AD 100, and were written by the people living in and around the fort of Vindolanda. The messages on them tell us a lot about life at the time. Some of them are messages about **trade** or business but there are also fun messages. Hundreds of tablets have been found at Vindolanda and experts are working all the time to understand what they say about Roman life.

This surviving tablet from Vindolanda is an invitation to a birthday party! It was sent from Claudia Severa to her friend Sulpicia Lepidina.

What is a milecastle?

Along the length of Hadrian's Wall, roughly a Roman mile apart, there are small forts, or fortlets, called milecastles. Milecastles were places where smaller groups of soldiers could live for a while. Some of the milecastles were built to protect a gateway in the wall. They would have been used to keep a close eye on who was coming and going through the gateways.

Milecastles are numbered from 1 to 80, from east to west. This is number 42.

Building the Milecastles

As with Hadrian's Wall, in the east the milecastles were originally made of wood and **turf**, but were later made stronger by rebuilding with stone. In the west they were built of stone from the beginning. They varied in size, but were generally about 15 metres

This cut-away illustration shows what a turret at Hadrian's Wall would have looked like.

by 15 metres, with walls of up to 6 metres high. The walls were very thick: some of them were up to 3 metres thick! Milecastles were square in shape.

Between each pair of milecastles there were two turrets that were around 9 metres tall. Inside the turret was a stair or ladder to the top. Historians believe this led to a viewing platform on the roof of the building. This would have been a good place to get a clear view of the landscape.

There are 80 known milecastles along the length of Hadrian's Wall, and 158 turrets.

Soldiers of the wall

When a place was conquered by the Romans, it became part of the Empire. When that happened, men from those countries became soldiers of Rome. The **legionnaires** based in the forts of Hadrian's Wall were from all over the Empire. There were **regiments** from Spain, France, Germany and even from as far away as Syria and North Africa. We know this because of **inscriptions** on stone plaques found along the wall that give the details of the regiments stationed there.

INFANTRY AND CAVALRY

Each regimental unit would have been made up of infantry (soldiers on foot) or **cavalry** (soldiers on horseback) and sometimes both. A unit contained up to 1,000 men. When not on patrol, most men would have been in the fort. Some soldiers would have been sent to fetch supplies further away.

In the cavalry barracks, the soldiers shared space with their horses as the stables were attached to their sleeping areas! It must have been very smelly.

Barracks in forts

In the forts, the soldiers slept in buildings called barracks. Barracks were divided into small living spaces. A fort would also have buildings for storing supplies. The fort **commander** had a large house where he lived and made plans with officers.

Barracks in milecastles

Most milecastles would only have had room for about eight soldiers to sleep in. Some of the milecastles have been found to have had fireplaces and ovens. This shows us soldiers would have been able to stay there for quite a long time.

A legionnaire's uniform was complicated and heavy. A soldier would have been expected to keep it in good condition at all times. In Britain, the soldiers also wore a heavy cloak over the uniform to keep them dry and warm.

Training

The unit spent most of their days training for battle. The soldiers had large areas in the forts for marching and for keeping up their fighting skills and fitness. When not training, the men were also doing repair work to roads and building new sections of the wall.

15

PATROLLING THE WALL

Patrolling the wall was done by legionnaires and **auxiliaries**. The legionnaires mainly lived in fortresses or camps miles away. The auxiliaries mainly lived in the milecastles and forts along the wall. They patrolled either on horseback or on foot. When soldiers were on patrol on the wall it would have often been dangerous. The northern winters were bitterly cold and the soldiers often faced attacks from enemy tribes.

At the time, Roman soldiers were some of the best trained soldiers in the ancient world. A Roman soldier could march over 30 kilometres (18.5 miles) a day in full armour and equipment. Daily life patrolling along the wall was far from easy, but a soldier would have been used to difficult conditions.

This is an artist's impression of what Hadrian's Wall would have looked like.

The weather in the north of Britain is often cold and wet. Many of the soldiers came from north-western Europe. The soldiers who came from the warmer European countries would have found the conditions very different from their homelands.

CUSTOMS AND CULTURES

There would have been lots of different languages spoken at the wall. Roman soldiers kept all sorts of customs and cultures from their own countries. Some of the soldiers had relationships with local women, and many soldiers' wives and children lived just outside the fort. This sort of **civilian settlement** is often called a military **vicus**. A vicus would have been a lively place. There were shops, meeting places, pubs, doctors, dentists and even places to get your fortune told! See page 22 to find out about life in a vicus.

Fast Fact!

The Roman **emperors** knew how important their soldiers were so they built many things to make life easier for them. At the forts they had baths, decent places to sleep and even flushing toilets! The soldiers **traded** with local tribes and farmers and they were well fed.

17

Letter from a Roman soldier

Roman soldiers were away from home from many years. They would have stayed in touch with their families by writing letters. They may have written a letter like this:

My dearest father,

We have settled well after our long march here from the fort at Isca. Not all of the Legio Secunda Augusta have joined us. Some were lucky enough to be left behind. I say "lucky" because our time here is even harder than at Isca. I wish that I had never complained about the (drilling) and the hard work! Here we are all either building, digging or on patrol.

The natives lack our culture and, compared to me, seem dressed in little more than rags, but they seem harmless enough. Some of them are even quite friendly and they bring their goods to the forts for trade. There are times when we are all grateful for their supplies and their skills at leatherwork. I am still not very good at mending my own kit, and a (leatherworker) in the vicus at Vindolanda has been a great help.

There is truth in the stories of the cold and wet, though. This is definitely not Hispania! The barracks are crowded and smelly, and one of the men in my contuburnium snores like a bear. With eight of us sharing it is not easy to sleep. The rain can set in for days and, at night, when we patrol along the dark stretches of the wall, it is hard to remember home at all. I am thankful for my wool birrus. Send extra socks and warmer subligacula in your next parcel!

Your devoted son, Marcus

DRILLING

Soldiers would have spent a lot of their time drilling. Drilling is marching and practising fighting methods over and over again. The Empire wanted their soldiers to be fit and ready to fight at all times.

LEATHERWORKERS

A Roman soldier had to take care of all of his own equipment. There is evidence of lots of different types of workers in the vicus, including people who repaired kit for the soldiers.

TALK LIKE A ROMAN!

birrus thick, woollen cloak with a hood

contuburnium group of eight legionnaire soldiers

Hispania modern Spain

Isca the main fort of the Legio Secunda Augusta in Wales

Legio Secunda Augusta one of the Roman legions in Britain

subligacula Roman underpants! One of the Vindolanda tablets really was a letter asking for extra socks and underpants.

Life for Britons near the wall

Britons lived along the whole length of Hadrian's Wall, but what was life really like for those who lived so close to the Romans? The Romans had **occupied** Britain for about 100 years by the time Hadrian's Wall was built. While many tribes regularly fought with the Romans, most people had been forced to adjust to life alongside them.

TRADE

Many tribes relied on the Romans for **trade**. The forts of the **Northern Frontier** were already places of trade, and **settlements** had grown along the length of the Roman roads long before the wall was built.

Tribes along the wall provided the Romans with goods such as meat, grain and leather.

TAXES

Archaeologists have found evidence of thousands of historic features from the time of the Romans. These include the remains of settlements, farms and mines that once belonged to British peoples. Some historians believe that for many tribes, the wall was an opportunity. It meant that they could trade more easily with the wealthy Romans. The local traders would have paid money to the Romans in the form of **taxes**. The Romans would have taken a percentage of the money that the local traders made from selling their goods. The Romans may also have taken a fee for passing safely through the gates of the wall.

Items like these Roman shoes help us to build up a picture of the lives of the people who lived near the wall during the Roman occupation of Britain.

Just outside the fort at Vindolanda there was a very large settlement. Here people lived and worked.

LIFE IN A VICUS

The **vicus** may also have been home to many Britons. They would have been craftspeople or traders, and people who worked alongside the fort in trades connected to leisure. Thousands of women would also have lived near the Roman forts. Many of these women would be the wives of the soldiers. There would also have been many children, as these were sons and daughters of the soldiers and the Britons working around the forts. We know that women and children lived at the vicus because archaeological evidence like tombstones, hairpins, women's jewellery and children's toys have been found.

Busy Lives!

The growth of the vicus would have meant a huge change in the lives of the tribespeople around the wall. Even if they did not live in the vicus, the local people may have visited to trade goods in the marketplace, or to enjoy Roman luxuries such as baths. For many people, life in the vicus was good, as they would have had access to benefits such as education and medicine. They would also have been able to buy luxury goods such as wine and olives. Next time you visit a busy market, imagine everyone in Roman clothing and you will get an idea of what the crowded vicus was like!

This picture shows the remains of a hypocaust from one of the buildings at Vindolanda. A hypocaust was a system of underfloor heating.

Letter from a Briton

Roman soldiers were allowed to marry Britons. Their families would have lived in the **settlements** close to the forts. This might be the kind of letter that the daughter of a **legionnaire** based in Britain would write to her father's relatives in Rome.

Salve, dearest cousin Flavia!

I am so excited that you and your father are coming to visit. My brother secretly told me that the men are going to the shrine of Mithras. We can spend time together when they are busy! I am offering votives for the weather to stay fine enough for the roads to stay open. Father has bought in enough liquamen to last the whole winter, in case the snow comes. The smell is everywhere.

My mother is not hiding the fact that she does not like these new Roman Gods, but she did marry a Roman legionnaire. I am happy to give praise to as many Gods as necessary if it means that you can visit! Mother has a shrine in the house for her British Gods, and so does Father for the Roman ones. Sometimes it feels like they spend all their time at a lararium.

I had better finish my letter now, as my brother will be home from his tutor soon. I do wish that I was allowed to have schooling. Anything would be better than a day filled with household chores. I would love to learn more than just reading and writing. All I am allowed to learn is how to sew and cook and clean. Life is so boring here for a girl.

I am so looking forward to seeing you again. Bring all the news from the forum of Rome, and maybe one day I will be allowed to visit the land of my father's birth too.

Yours, Regina

Girls' education

In the Roman Empire, girls were not expected to go to school. Instead they learnt at home. Girls were also expected to help around the home. They learnt how to cook, clean and sew. Girls were expected to marry a man of their parents' choosing from around the age of 12.

Talk like a Roman!

forum open public space in Roman cities where people met to talk

lararium small household altar to the Gods

liquamen a very stinky fish sauce that Romans loved

Mithras one of the Gods of Rome, worshipped by a secretive group of men

salve hello

votives small objects offered as gifts to the Gods

Hadrian's Wall after the Romans

Roman control of Britain stopped in AD 410, and gradually the wall was abandoned. It fell into **disrepair**. Most of its stone was used by local people to build houses, churches and even castles. During the 1800s, **conservation** groups began to protect and look after what was left of the ruins. In some places, the wall was even rebuilt. At sites such as Vindolanda, there are wonderful **reconstructions** of milecastles and we can even read the words of the people who lived there.

THE WALL IN RUINS

In many places, remains of the milecastles and forts are still standing. These ruins give us a feel for the size of the original buildings. We can easily see just how thick the walls were and how strong

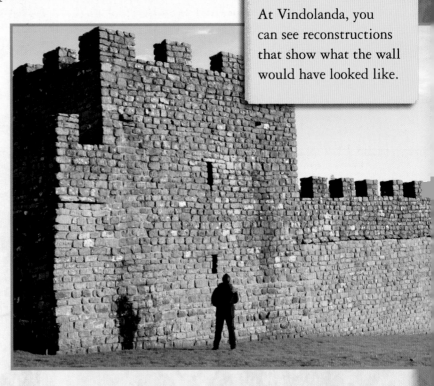

At Vindolanda, you can see reconstructions that show what the wall would have looked like.

they must have been. Most of the milecastles were quite a long march from the nearest fort, and these small buildings would have become home to the soldiers stationed there. To protect the ruins, the wall was named a World Heritage Site in 1987.

Even today the remains of Hadrian's Wall are very impressive. They show us how powerful the Romans were.

TURNING BACK TIME

Visiting Hadrian's Wall and the forts built along it is like stepping back in time. While the wall itself may have crumbled, there are sections where very little has changed in the landscape. During Roman times, there would have been lots of through traffic along the wall. Even without all the people, we can still imagine what life must have been like for a Roman soldier a long way from home, stationed on the cold and windswept wall, watching out for attack from enemy tribes.

Timeline

BC

55 BC
Julius Caesar and his army try but fail to **invade** Britain

54 BC
Julius Caesar and his army try again to invade Britain

AD

AD 43
Emperor Claudius successfully invades Britain

AD 70
The Romans spread to northern Britain and start building roads and forts

AD 100
Roman army placed in forts along the **Northern Frontier**

AD 117
Emperor Trajan dies and Hadrian becomes the new emperor of Rome

AD 121
Emperor Hadrian orders the building of a wall in Britain, marking the Northern Frontier

AD 122
Emperor Hadrian visits Britain and inspects the building of the wall

AD 140s
Hadrian's Wall is mostly finished

AD 180–AD 200
Military **settlements** ("vici") grow around the Roman forts, and new settlements spread along the length of the wall

Late 3rd and early 4th century AD
Tribal uprisings along the Northern Frontier lead to the wall being attacked

AD 410
The Romans abandon Britain

5th–17th century AD
The stones of Hadrian's Wall are used by local people in their buildings

18th–19th century AD
Conservation groups begin to protect and save the remains of the wall

1987
Hadrian's Wall declared a World Heritage Site

Glossary

altar raised platform or table used in religious customs

aqueduct bridge built to carry water over a river or valley

auxiliary supporting soldier who is not a citizen of the Roman Empire

barracks buildings in the forts where the soldiers stayed

cavalry soldiers on horseback

civilian person who is not a member of the army

commander person who is in charge of soldiers or a group of people

conservation protection or rebuilding of a natural environment

dedicated something that is set apart for a special use or purpose

defensive structure building, wall or place built to protect the people within it from enemies

disrepair when a building is in poor condition because nobody has looked after it

earthwork large bank of earth

emperor ruler or head of an empire

excavate uncover something by digging or removing soil

inscription carving in stone or wood that gives details of past people or events

invade take over a country or place by force

legion Roman army unit made up of both soldiers on foot and horseback

legionnaire member of a Roman legion

Northern Frontier border or edge of territory at the most northern part of the Roman Empire; this was at Hadrian's Wall

occupy take over and use land or a place by military force

rebel fight against the government or ruling power of a country

reconstruction recreating or rebuilding a past building or event using evidence of what it was like at the time

regiment large group of soldiers within a unit

settlement place where a group of people have made their homes and created a community

tax sum of money paid to a government or ruling body

territory land belonging to a group of people or a country

threat likely cause of danger

trade buy or sell goods and services

turf surface of the soil that is held together by grass and plant roots

vallum deep ditches and earthworks that the Romans built on the southern side of the wall

vicus (plural "vici") settlement beside Hadrian's Wall where Britons lived, including the families of Roman soldiers

Find out more

BOOKS

Life in Roman Britain (A Child's History of Britain), Anita Ganeri (Raintree, 2014)

Roman Sites (Historic Places of the United Kingdom), John Malam (Raintree, 2018)

The Roman Empire and its Impact on Britain (Early British History), Claire Throp (Raintree, 2016)

The Roman Tribune (Newspapers from History), Andrew Langley (Raintree, 2018)

WEBSITES

You can read all about the Roman Empire on this BBC site:
www.bbc.co.uk/education/topics/zwmpfg8

The Vindolanda official website has lots of information for children:
www.vindolanda.com

PLACES TO VISIT

There are many sites along the length of the Hadrian's Wall. Today, you can visit museums, forts, bathhouses, turrets, shrines and even the remains of Roman towns. See the official website for Hadrian's Wall Country for details of all the key sites, and how you can visit them: **hadrianswallcountry.co.uk**

Chesters Roman Fort is a well-preserved Roman cavalry fort. Here, you can get a taste of what life was like for the cavalry soldiers. There is a wonderfully preserved bathhouse and steam room and a large collection of inscribed altar stones.

Chesters Roman Fort and Museum
Chollerford, Hexham,
Northumberland NE46 4EU

Roman Vindolanda is one of the most important Roman
archaeological sites in Europe. The remains of the fort and
vicus let us get a better understanding of what life was like
during Roman times. The museum has a large collection of
the Vindolanda tablets, so we can see the actual words of the
Romans who once lived there.

Roman Vindolanda
Chesterholm Museum
Bardon Mill, Hexham,
Northumberland NE47 7JN

The Roman Army Museum is the best place to find out what
life was like for a Roman soldier.

Roman Army Museum
Carvoran House,
Brampton, Greenhead,
Cumbria CA8 7JB

Housesteads Roman Fort is open all year round. It is set
high up on a rocky ridge. From here, you can get a real feel of
how wild and windswept the landscape around the wall can
be. There is also a well-preserved example of a row of Roman
toilets. A loo with a view!

Housesteads Roman Fort and Museum
Haydon Bridge
Hexham
Northumberland NE47 6NN

Index

altars 10, 25, 30
Augusta, Emperor 4
auxiliaries 9, 16

barracks 14, 15, 18
baths and toilets 17, 23, 30, 31
Britons 4, 5, 9, 16, 17, 18, 20–25
building materials 9, 13

Caesar, Julius 4, 28
camps 5, 16
Castle Sant' Angelo 7
cavalry 14, 30
Chesters Roman Fort 30–31
children 17, 22
Claudius, Emperor 5, 28
clothes 18, 19
commanders 15
customs and cultures 17

drilling 18, 19

earthworks 8
education 23, 24, 25
emperors 4, 5, 6–7, 17, 28

forts 5, 7, 8, 9, 12–13, 14, 15, 16, 17, 20, 24, 26, 30–31

gates 12, 21

Hadrian, Emperor 5, 6–7, 28
Hadrian's Wall
    abandonment of 26, 28
    conservation of 26, 28
    construction 9
    excavations of 10
    map of 8
    reconstructions 9, 26
    World Heritage Site 26, 28
Housesteads Roman Fort 31
hypocausts 23

infantry 14
inscriptions 10, 14
invasions of Britain 4, 5, 28
Iron Age 4

leatherworkers 18, 19
legions and legionnaires 9, 14, 15, 16, 19, 24
letter writing 11, 18, 24
liquamen (fish sauce) 24, 25

map of Hadrian's Wall 8
map of the Roman Empire (AD 117) 5
marriage 17, 24, 25
milecastles 8, 9, 12–13, 15, 16, 26
Mithras 24, 25

Northern Frontier 7, 9, 20, 28

patrols 16, 18

reconstructions 9, 26
religion 24, 25
roads 5
Roman Army Museum 31
Roman Empire 4, 5, 6, 7, 14, 25
roundhouses 4

Scotland 7
settlements, British 20, 21, 24
shoes 21
shrines 24
soldiers, Roman 4, 9, 12, 14–19

taxes 21
timeline 28
tombstones 10
trade 11, 17, 18, 20, 21, 22, 23
training, army 15, 19
Trajan, Emperor 6
tribes 4, 5, 9, 16, 17, 20, 23
turrets 13

vallum 8
vicus (civilian settlement) 17, 19, 22–23, 28
viewing platforms 13
Vindolanda 9, 22, 26, 31
Vindolanda tablets 11, 19, 31

weather 16, 17, 18
women and girls 17, 22, 24, 25